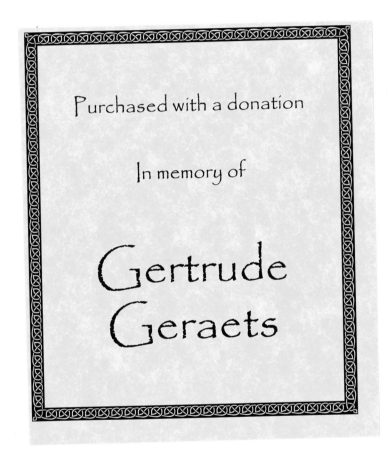

Purchased with a donation

In memory of

Gertrude
Geraets

Mechanic Mike's Machines

Rescue Machines

A+
Smart Apple Media

Published by Smart Apple Media, an imprint of Black Rabbit Books
P.O. Box 3263, Mankato, Minnesota 56002
www.blackrabbitbooks.com

Produced by David West Children's Books
6 Princeton Court, 55 Felsham Road, London SW15 1AZ

Designed and illustrated by David West

Copyright © 2014 David West Children's Books

Library of Congress Cataloging-in-Publication Data

West, David, 1956-
Rescue vehicles / David West.
     pages cm – (Mechanic Mike's machines)
Includes index.
Audience: Grades K to 3.
ISBN 978-1-62588-058-1 (library binding)
ISBN 978-1-62588-097-0 (paperback)
1. Emergency vehicles–Juvenile literature. 2. Rescue work–Juvenile literature. I. Title.
TL235.8.W47 2015
629.225–dc23
                                           2013032024

Printed in China
CPSIA compliance information: DWCB14CP
010114

9 8 7 6 5 4 3 2 1

JUV
629.225
WES

Mechanic Mike says:
This little guy will tell
you something more
about the machine.

Find out what type
of engine drives
the machine.

Discover
something you
didn't know.

Is it fast or slow?
Top speeds are
given here.

How many people
operate it?

Get your
amazing
fact here!

Contents

Police Car

Police cars are used to reach the scene of an incident quickly, to transport criminal suspects, or to patrol an area.

Some police forces use fast cars such as Porsches as pursuit cars.

 The Holden Monaro can go from 0 to 100 mph (160 km/h) in 4.8 seconds.

 Police cars usually patrol with two officers.

 Did you know that police cars use flashing lights and sirens when there is an emergency?

 This car has a **supercharged** 5.7 -liter gasoline engine.

Mechanic Mike says:
The Australian police use this Holden Monaro muscle car as a pursuit car as well as everyday work. The bright paint work makes the car easy to see.

This Type III ambulance has a 6.8-liter gasoline engine.

Did you know that horse-drawn ambulances were first used by Napoleon's Army of the Rhine in 1793?

Ambulances usually have a crew of two—a driver with medical training and a **paramedic**.

Ambulances must be able to cruise at a speed of 65 mph (105 km/h) and be able to pass vehicles at 70 mph (113 km/h).

The first motorized ambulance was first used in Chicago in February, 1899.

Ambulance

Ambulances can be used to rush to the scene of an emergency. They use flashing lights and sirens to warn people of their approach.

Mechanic Mike says:
In the back of the ambulance is the mobile intensive care unit. Patients are cared for until the ambulance gets them to a hospital.

Fire Engine

Fire engines don't just put out fires. This turntable ladder fire engine can rescue people trapped in the upper levels of tall buildings.

Not all fire engines have ladders. Some carry water and hoses so that they can spray water onto the fire.

Fire engines are limited to 75 mph (121 km/h).

This fire engine has a crew of three firefighters.

Did you know a turntable ladder can extend to 98.5 feet (30 m)? That means it can reach as high as the 13th floor of a building.

Fire engines are powered by **diesel engines**.

Mechanic Mike says:
Turntable ladder fire engines have telescopic ladders that can extend.

9

Tow Truck

Emergency road services send out tow trucks to rescue motorists that have broken down. If the vehicle cannot be repaired at the road side, it will be towed to the nearest garage.

Mechanic Mike says:
Tow trucks are also called wreckers.

Most tow trucks have a winch to pull the vehicle onto the back of a flat bed.

Although they have powerful engines, their maximum speed is around 56 mph (90 km/h).

These trucks are usually operated by one person.

Tow trucks use diesel engines as they have better pulling power than gasoline engines. Trucks like this one have 12-liter engines. That's over 3 gallons!

Did you know that massive tow trucks like this one can tow large, heavy vehicles like trucks and buses?

This Honda motorcycle has an 1084 cc gasoline engine.

Did you know paramedic motorcycles have flashing lights and sirens just like police cars and ambulances?

A paramedic motorcycle carries only one person.

This Honda ST1100 has a top speed of 134 mph (215.6 km/h).

Some motorcycles have sidecars to carry injured people to a hospital.

Mechanic Mike says:
Paramedic motorcycles are also known as motorcycle ambulances.

12

Motorcycle

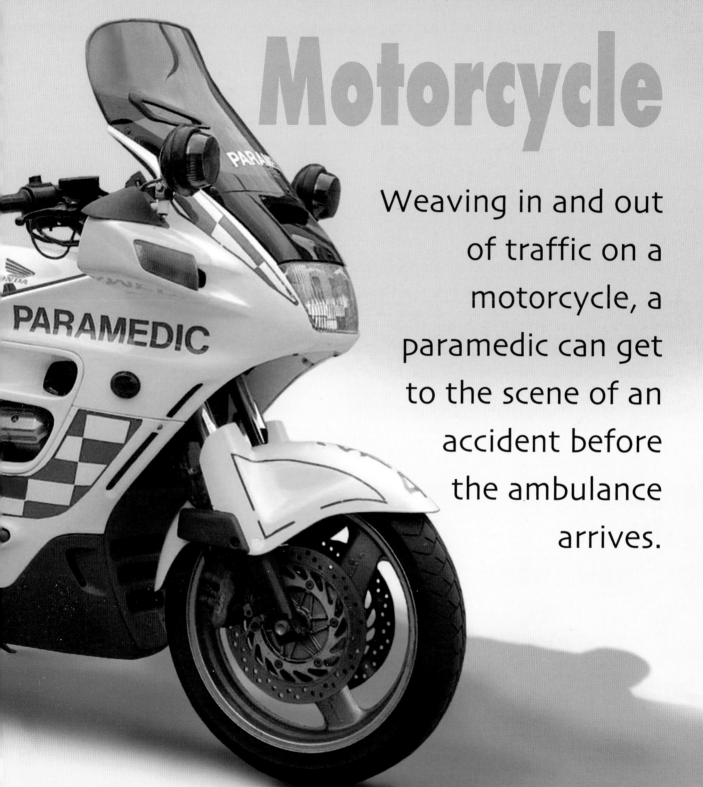

Weaving in and out of traffic on a motorcycle, a paramedic can get to the scene of an accident before the ambulance arrives.

Air Ambulance

Sometimes it is necessary to get to a sick or injured person where an ambulance or motorcycle cannot go. Helicopter air ambulances can reach people on mountains and in other areas of rough terrain.

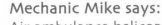

Mechanic Mike says:
Air ambulance helicopters are also used in cities where accidents may have blocked the roads with traffic so a truck ambulance cannot get to the site.

G-DORS

Helicopters can land and take off vertically.

Did you know that ambulance helicopters were first used by the US army during the Korean War (1950–53).

This helicopter can cruise at 140 mph (226 km/h).

Air ambulances usually have a pilot and one or two-person crew.

These helicopters use **turboshaft** engines to power the rotor blades.

Mountain Rescue

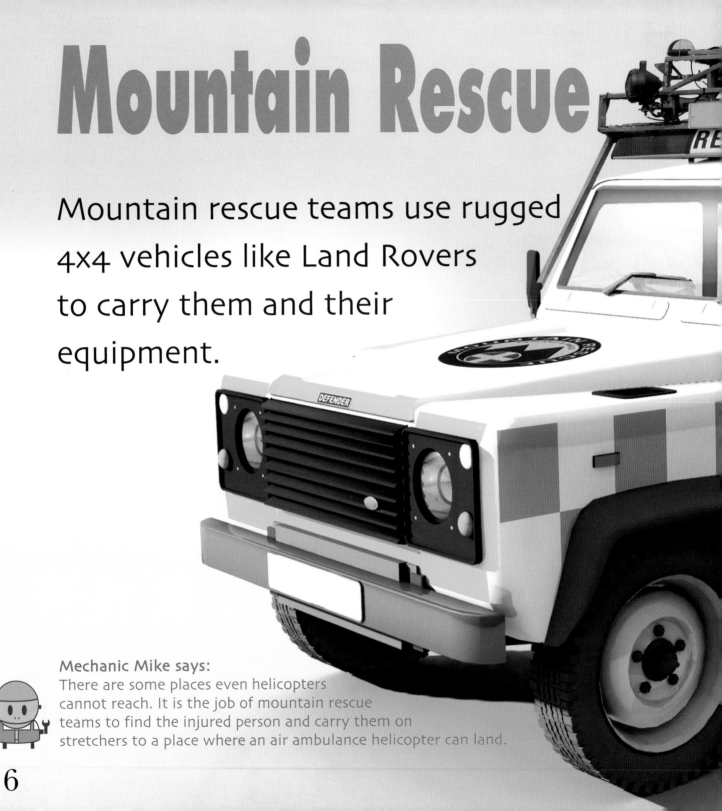

Mountain rescue teams use rugged 4x4 vehicles like Land Rovers to carry them and their equipment.

Mechanic Mike says:
There are some places even helicopters cannot reach. It is the job of mountain rescue teams to find the injured person and carry them on stretchers to a place where an air ambulance helicopter can land.

BRECON MOUNTAIN RESCUE

Vehicles like these use **turbo-charged** diesel engines.

Did you know that mountain rescue teams sometimes use dogs to help find injured climbers?

This 4x4 can carry up to seven people plus equipment.

Although they have a top speed of around 100 mph (161 km/h), these vehicles are designed to travel at much lower speeds.

Vehicles with four wheel drive (4x4) are able to travel over rough terrain as all four wheels are being powered by the engine.

Lifeboat

People in trouble at sea close to shore are rescued by lifeboats like this RIB (Rigid Inflatable Boat). RIBs are easily steered through shallow water and rough waves.

Did you know that, if it capsizes, an inflatable bag flips it back the right way?

These lifeboats can travel at a speed of 33 mph (53 km/h).

There is a helmsman (driver) and two crew members.

It has two outboard motors with propellers.

It can run at full speed for three hours.

RESCUE

Port Alice

PORTABLE RADAR TRANSMITTER

19

The Sikorsky HH-60J has radar for searching that gives its nose a distinctive look.

Did you know the hoist on the left hand side can lift people from 200 ft (61.0 m) below?

The Sikorsky HH-60 Jayhawk is capable of reaching 207 mph (333 km/h) for short periods. It can fly at 161 mph (259 km/h) for six to seven hours.

This helicopter has a crew of four. It can hoist up to six additional people on board.

It has two turboshaft engines powering the rotor blades.

DANGER
KEEP AWAY

DANGER
7538

U. S.
COAST GUARD

Coast Guard

Coast Guard helicopters perform search and rescue around the coast, from rescuing people who have slipped off cliffs to saving crews from sinking ships.

Mechanic Mike says:
The Sikorsky HH-60J is normally based on land but can also operate from Coast Guard ships.

Some countries' armed forces use large, modified airliners as flying hospitals to transfer patients long distances.

Did you know that the first air ambulances were modified biplanes during World War I?

The Beechcraft Super King Air can cruise at 316 mph (509 km/h).

Generally there are at least two medical crew members in addition to the pilot.

This plane has two **turboprop** engines.

Mechanic Mike says:
The Royal Flying Doctor Service of Australia is one of the largest air ambulance organizations in the world. It is known as the "Flying Doctor."

VH-MSH

Flying Doctor

As well as helicopters, light planes are also used as air ambulances. They are essential in places like Australia, where some people live in remote regions.

Glossary

diesel engines
Engines using diesel fuel.

paramedic
A medically trained person who works in emergency situations.

turbo-charged
Extra power supplied to the engine by a turbine powered by exhaust gases.

turboprop
An engine similar to a jet that turns a propeller.

turboshaft
An engine similar to a turbo prop but instead it turns a shaft.

supercharged
Extra power supplied to an engine by a supercharger.

Index

10.15